Bookworms

Creepy Crawlers

Caterpillars

Anika Abraham

Cavendish Square
New York

Published in 2019 by Cavendish Square Publishing, LLC
243 5th Avenue, Suite 136, New York, NY 10016

First Edition

Website: cavendishsq.com

Library of Congress Cataloging-in-Publication Data

Names: Abraham, Anika, author.
Title: Caterpillars / Anika Abraham.
Description: First edition. | New York : Cavendish Square, [2019] |
Series: Creepy crawlers | Audience: Grades K-3. | Includes bibliographical references and index.
Identifiers: LCCN 2018018902 (print) | LCCN 2018021791 (ebook) | ISBN 9781502641717 (ebook) |
ISBN 9781502641700 (library bound) | ISBN 9781502641687 (pbk) | ISBN 9781502641694 (6 pack)
Subjects: LCSH: Caterpillars--Juvenile literature.
Classification: LCC QL544.2 (ebook) | LCC QL544.2 .A27 2019 (print) | DDC 595.7813/92--dc23
LC record available at https://lccn.loc.gov/2018018902

Editorial Director: David McNamara
Editor: Kristen Susienka
Copy Editor: Nathan Heidelberger
Associate Art Director: Alan Sliwinski
Designer: Megan Metté
Production Coordinator: Karol Szymczuk
Photo Research: J8 Media

The photographs in this book are used by permission and through the courtesy of: Cover Denis Vesely/Shutterstock.com; p. 5 Sandra Standbridge/Moment/Getty Images; p. 7 Dorling Kindersley/Getty Images; p. 9 108MotionBG/Shutterstock.com; p. 11 Cathy Keifer/Shutterstock.com; p. 13 Chekaramit/Shutterstock.com; p. 15 Ruth Swan/Shutterstock.com; p. 17 Neil Bromhall/Shutterstock.com; p. 19 Raquel Lonas/Moment/Getty Images; p. 21 Chain Foto24/Shutterstock.com.

Printed in the United States of America

Contents

A Caterpillar's Life **4**

New Words **22**

Index **23**

About the Author **24**

Caterpillars look creepy!

They can have long bodies.

They can have short bodies.

Caterpillars grow inside an egg.

They eat the egg to leave it.

Caterpillars eat a lot.

They like to eat leaves
or grass.

They live close to their food.

Caterpillars **shed** their skin.

Some caterpillars shed their skin five times.

A caterpillar's body is soft and squishy.

Caterpillars can be many colors.

Caterpillars have six legs.

They also have other parts that look like legs.

These are called **prolegs**.

They are not real legs.

Some caterpillars hide
from **predators**.

Their colors help them hide.

Caterpillars change into butterflies or moths.

They do this by **metamorphosis**.

Butterflies and moths
look very different
from caterpillars.

Can you see any caterpillars
or butterflies near you?

New Words

metamorphosis (met-ah-MORE-fo-sis) The steps a caterpillar takes to change into a butterfly or moth.

predators (PRED-uh-torz) Animals or insects that want to eat or hurt other animals or insects.

prolegs (PRO-legz) Parts of a caterpillar's body that act as legs but are not real legs. They are in the middle of its body.

shed (SHED) To remove.

Index

bodies, 4, 12

butterflies, 18, 20

colors, 12, 16

eat, 6, 8

egg, 6

metamorphosis, 18

moths, 18, 20

predators, 16

prolegs, 14

shed, 10

About the Author

Anika Abraham enjoys the outdoors. She likes learning and writing about animals, insects, and plants. She lives in Chicago, Illinois, with her cat Scrooge and her dog Thunder.

About BOOKWORMS

Bookworms help independent readers gain reading confidence through high-frequency words, simple sentences, and strong picture/text support. Each book explores a concept that helps children relate what they read to the world they live in.